GORILLAS

designed and written by Althea

illustrated by Barbara McGirr

Longman Group USA Inc.

Published in the United States of America by Longman Group USA Inc.
© 1987, 1988 Althea Braithwaite

Originally published in Great Britain in a slightly altered form by Longman Group UK Limited

ISBN: 0-88462-170-7 (library bound)
ISBN: 0-88462-171-5 (paperback)

Printed in the United States of America

88 89 90 10 9 8 7 6 5 4 3 2 1

Library of Congress Cataloging-in-Publication Data

Althea.
  Gorillas.

  (Save our wildlife)
  1. Gorillas--Juvenile literature. I. McGirr, Barbara. II. Title. III. Series:
Althea. Save our wildlife.
QL737.P96A38 1988   599.88   88-26655
ISBN 0-88462-170-7
ISBN 0-88462-171-5 (pbk.)

Notes for parents and teachers
Save Our Wildlife books have been specially written and designed as a simple, yet informative, series of factual nature books for young children.

The illustrations are bright and clear, and children can "read" the pictures while the story is read to them.

The text has been specially set in large type to make it easy for children to follow along or even to read for themselves.

As it begins to get light
the gorillas wake up.
Yawning, they stretch themselves
and climb sleepily out of their nests
to go in search of something to eat.

Gorillas live in family groups.
The leader is a strong, old male
called a silverback.
Three or four females and
their young live with the male.

Each of the mothers
has a baby every
five years or so.
The old leader, helped by young
males, looks after the family.
Up to twelve gorillas live together.

The group breakfasts on leaves, nettles, thistles and bamboo. They also like to eat flower buds and berries. Gorillas get most of the water they need from eating plants such as wild celery.

After their first big meal,
the group will wander
slowly along, eating a plant
or two as they go.

Gorillas walk on all fours,
but a mother has to carry her baby,
using one arm to clutch it
to her chest.
When it is about four months old,
it will ride on her back.

Baby gorillas learn to crawl
at about nine weeks.
They can't walk until they
are eight or nine months old.

A baby starts eating leaves,
but it doesn't stop drinking
milk from its mother until
it is a year and a half old.

The young gorilla shares
its mother's sleeping nest
until she has another baby.

After the group has a midday meal
the gorillas rest. They settle down
around their silverback leader.
Feeling good on a warm sunny day,
they make purring noises
at one another.

The older animals want to rest, but
the young ones start to play.
The adults may grunt at them to
settle down again.

The young ones like sliding
down slopes or covering themselves
with large leaves.
They've even been seen playing
catch with a large round fruit.

They enjoy being tickled.
Sometimes the play gets too rough
and fighting begins.
Then the silverback may slap them
lightly on the back to stop them.

Other gorillas in the group
help to look after the young ones.
Older females help a mother
cuddle and groom her baby,
combing its hair.

When the males and females are
grown up and adults, they leave
the group to go off on their own.
They may try to join another group,
or a male will start a group
of his own.

When two groups of gorillas meet,
they may spend time together without
anything happening.
But if an older gorilla feels his group
is in danger or if the new group
tries to take one of his females,
the silverback gets angry.
Sometimes there will be trouble.

When he is angry, a male gorilla
roars and swells out his chest.
He beats his chest with his hands.

Then he drops down on all fours
and moves forward, screaming
and throwing branches.
This is often frightening enough
to stop the fight before it starts.

Soon the leaders of the two groups
go off in different directions, as if
nothing had happened.

When evening comes,
the gorillas have
their last meal of the day
and find a place to rest
for the night.

The young ones build their nests
up in the branches of trees.
The older, heavier gorillas
make their nests on the ground.

The silverback may share a nest
with one of the older females.
They settle down to sleep,
sometimes snoring gently.

Gorillas are the largest of the great apes. A male can weigh more than 450 pounds and stand as high as five feet tall. But for all their size and strength, gorillas are usually described as peaceful and gentle. They are plant eaters and live in the mountain and lowland forests of West Africa.

Unlike chimpanzees, gorillas walk on all fours. Their arms are longer than their legs, and in walking their weight is put on their knuckles and feet. They rarely stand erect, usually only when threatened. Because they are heavy, the adults are not tree dwellers and feed on the ground.

Gorillas live in family groups, each with its own territory. They roam during the day, seeking food, and have no permanent home. Instead, they build new sleeping nests wherever they stop at night. Young gorillas no longer with their mothers make nests in trees, but the adults remain on the ground.

While females have the primary care of babies and youngsters, males play with them and sometimes discipline misbehavior. A gorilla matures in about half the time a human child requires. In captivity, gorillas have lived to be fifty years old, but life span can only be guessed at for those in the wild.

The clearing of forests and the killing of gorillas by poachers threaten to destroy these magnificent animals. There will always be a need for protected forest areas for this endangered species, already severely reduced in numbers.